SUPERSTARS OF BASEBALL

NELSON CRUZ

THE RISE TO THE TOP!

Cruz is a baseball star that breaks records!

2012

Cruz and the Rangers play in the World Series.

2010 AND 2011

Cruz is traded to the Texas Rangers.

2006

Cruz starts playing in the Major Leagues.

2005

Cruz starts playing in the minor leagues.

2001

The Mets trade Cruz to the Oakland Athletics.

2000

The New York Mets sign a contract with Nelson.

1998

Nelson Cruz is born in Monte Cristi in the Dominican Republic.

1980

Mason Crest
370 Reed Road
Broomall, Pennsylvania 19008
www.masoncrest.com

Printed and bound in the United States of America.

First printing
9 8 7 6 5 4 3 2 1

Library of Congress Cataloging-in-Publication Data

Rodríguez Gonzalez, Tania.
 Nelson Cruz / by Tania Rodriguez.
     p. cm.
 Includes index.
 ISBN 978-1-4222-2691-9 (hardcover)-- ISBN 978-1-4222-2670-4 (series hardcover)--
 ISBN 978-1-4222-9180-1 (ebook)
 1. Cruz, Nelson, 1980- 2. Hispanic American baseball players--Biography--Juvenile
literature. 3. Baseball players--United States--Biography--Juvenile literature. I. Title.
 GV865.C78R64 2012
 796.357092--dc23
 [B]

                              2012021367

Produced by Harding House Publishing Services, Inc.
www.hardinghousepages.com

NELSON CRUZ

Chapter 1

BASEBALL, THE DOMINICAN REPUBLIC, AND NELSON CRUZ

In the last few years, Nelson Cruz has become one of baseball's rising stars. He has done amazing things in his time in the MLB. He's played in the World Series. He's played in the *All-Star game*.

In 2011, he won the American League Championship Series Most Valuable Player award. Cruz's amazing play in the 2011 ALCS broke more than one record. No player has ever hit more home runs or had more *RBIs* in a postseason series than Cruz, and only Cruz has ever hit a walk-off grand slam in the postseason. Every player dreams of doing the things that Cruz has done.

Today, Cruz is living his dream. He's playing baseball in the *MLB* and finding success. But Cruz had to work hard for years to make that dream come true. He's come a long way from

his hometown in the Dominican Republic! But he's always brought his homeland with him during his long road to the Major Leagues. He knows that the Dominican Republic helped make him strong. The Dominican baseball *culture* helped Cruz become the player he is today. Great Dominican baseball players provided him with wonderful role models.

Ozzie Virgil

Ozzie was a Dominican baseball player who came to the United States in 1947 and started playing baseball with the U.S. Marines in the '50s. He was *signed* with the New York Giants in 1953, and he made the Major Leagues in 1956. Ozzie played with the Giants, the Tigers, the Pirates, the SF Giants, the Orioles, and the Kansas City A's. But Ozzie hadn't forgotten his homeland;

during the winter season, he played with the Águilas and Escojido in the Dominican Republic.

When Ozzie finally retired from being a player, he went to coaching, with the San Francisco Giants, the Expos, the Padres, and the Mariners. He also managed the Águilas and Escojido in the Dominican Republic.

Felipe Alou

The next big Dominican player was Felipe Alou. In 1966, Felipe was named first baseman on the Sporting News All-Stars Team; he led the National League in total bases, hits, and at bats while also hitting 31 homers. Felipe was known for speaking up for Hispanics in the baseball world.

Then, in 1979, Felipe became an Expos coach, and in 1992, he was named *manager* of the Expos. Two years later, in 1994, he was named Manager of the Year in the National League, and the next year he led the National League in the All-Stars game and took home the trophy.

Juan Marichal

Perhaps the most famous of all Big-League Dominican baseball players is Juan Marichal. He won more than 20

FELIPE ALOU
NEW YORK YANKEES   1st BASE

games in six out of seven consecutive seasons for San Francisco. He also tied a record for pitching in eight All-Stars Games, two of which he won in 1962 and 1964. During the 1960s, Juan dominated the National League, and in 1963, Marichal pitched a no-hitter; two weeks, later he and Warren Spahn battled for 16 innings in one of the greatest pitching match-ups of all time. Marichal won 1–0, on a home run by Willie Mays. In 1983, Juan Marichal made every Dominican proud by becoming the first to reach the Baseball Hall of Fame in Cooperstown, New York.

Julian Javier

With Javier's amazing play at second base, the Cardinals won three National League titles between 1964 and 1968, and the World Series against the Yankees in 1964 and then against the Red Sox in 1967. Javier's three-run homer in Game 7 of the 1967 World Series helped lock it up for the Cardinals. In four World Series he batted .333.

When he left the Big Leagues, he went back home to the Dominican Republic, where he managed the Águilas Cibaeñas.

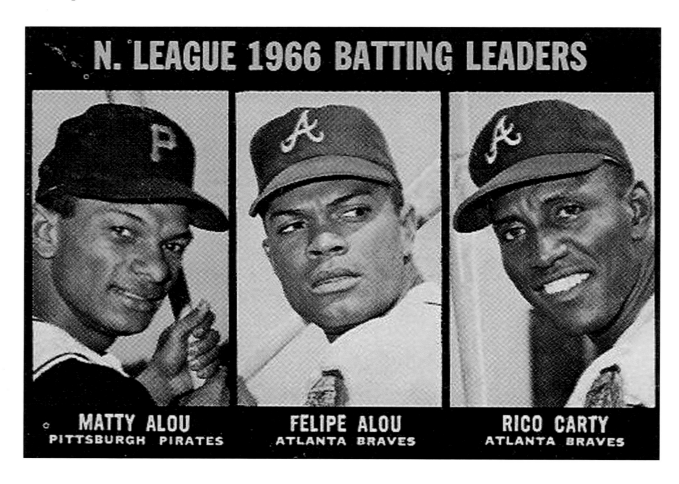

N. LEAGUE 1966 BATTING LEADERS

MATTY ALOU
PITTSBURGH PIRATES

FELIPE ALOU
ATLANTA BRAVES

RICO CARTY
ATLANTA BRAVES

Manny Mota

This Dominican player is the most accomplished pinch hitter in Major League history; he holds the record with 150 career pinch hits. He hit over .300 for the Dodgers in five consecutive seasons from 1969 to 1973, and then went back home to coach for the Dodgers in the Dominican Republic. Today, Manny Mota has four sons in *professional* baseball, and he owns a restaurant in Santo Domingo called Manny Mota's Dugout. He also operates the Manny Mota Youth League in the Dominican Republic.

Rico Carty

When Rico Carty started playing baseball, he was so impressive that ten different clubs signed him. Rico was one of the best natural hitters ever to play, but unfortunately, his career was sidetracked by illness and injury. He hit over .330 with 22 home runs in his *rookie* season (1964), and then he hit over .300 in three of his first four seasons. In 1968, however, he contracted tuberculosis and missed the entire season. He came in 1969, and hit and amazing .342. The next year, he won the batting title, but then he missed the entire 1971 season because of a knee injury. Rico never gave up, though. In 1979, he hit 31 home runs at the age of 39. Today, he holds the honorary rank of general in the Dominican Army.

Matty Alou

Felipe's brother Matty proved the baseball skill ran in the Alou family. Matty won the batting title in 1966 with .342; he posted a .338, .332, and .331 between 1967 and 1969. He even set a Major League record 698 official at-bats, and he retired with a .307 *batting average*.

César Cedeño

César Cedeño earned 5 consecutive Gold Gloves (1972–76) and appeared in the 1972–74 All Stars Game. In his rookie year, he hit .310 in 90 games; he also hit .320 in 1972 and 1973. In 1974, he drove 100 runs, and he stole 50 or more bases during six consecutive seasons (1972–77).

Jesús Alou

Felipe and Matty's brother carried on the family baseball *heritage*. And on 10 September 1963, Jesús, Matty, and Felipe Alou all batted against the New York Mets in the same inning, the only time three Major League brothers have ever stepped up to the plate in the same inning!

Between 1963 and 1979, Jesús had 82 pinch hits. His biggest day was on July 10,

1964, when he went six-for-six with five singles and a homer. In 1979, the Astros made Jesús a player-coach, and later he became a scout for the Montreal system in the Dominican Republic.

César Gerónimo

Three-time Gold Glove center fielder, César was one of the defensive stars of Cincinnati "Big Red Machine," a team best known for its hitting. He won his first Gold Glove in 1974, and he led the National League in putouts, total chances, and double plays in 1975.

Pedro Borbón

Whenever the Big Red Machine needed to shut down the opposition in the late innings, Pedro Borbón was the one they called. His first good year came in 1973, when he led the league in relief runs and was named to the All-Star team for the first of his four times. He compiled a lifetime 0.63 ERA in the *playoffs*, and he never yielded an earned run in seven games from 1973 to 1976. His son Pedro, Jr. grew up to also play professional baseball.

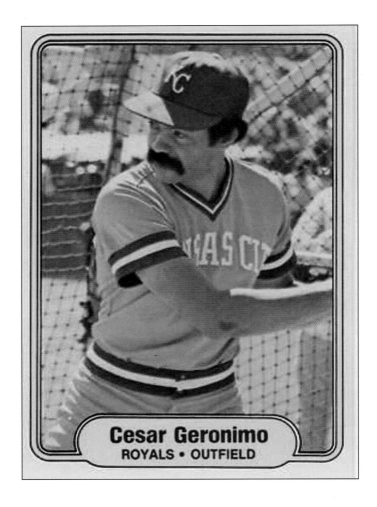

Cesar Geronimo
ROYALS • OUTFIELD

Pedro Guerrero

When Pedro was healthy, he was one of the best hitters in baseball. In 1981, he was hitting .300 with 12 homers and 48 RBIs. Later that year, in the World Series against the Yankees, he hit two homers and drove in seven runs, five in the final game. He shared the Series *MVP* Award with Ron Cey and Steve Garvey. In 1982, he hit .304 with 32 homers and 100 RBIs. The next season he had .298 with 32 homers and 103 RBIs. He missed part of 1984 and 1985 due to injuries, but he still managed to bring in 49 home runs in both seasons. In June of 1985, Pedro hit 16 home runs to tie the Major League records (along with Babe Ruth, Roger Maris, and Bob Johnson). He also approached a Major League record by reaching base 14 times in a row (two homers, three doubles, two singles, six walks, and a hit-by-pitch), two short of Ted Williams's mark. After another injury in 1986, though, Pedro was out of the game once again. But he still didn't give up; in 1987, he had his best year, batting .338 with 27 homers. Pedro retired in 1992.

Dominican Baseball Today

Players like these inspired new generations of Dominican boys, boys like Nelson Cruz who dreamed of growing up to be the next Alou or Moto.

And today, many baseball players from the Dominican Republic come to play in the United States. By 2011, a total of 420 players from the Dominican Republic had played in the Major Leagues. More Dominicans play in the Majors than players from any other country in Latin America. In fact, the Dominican Republic has more players in the Majors than all other countries in Latin America combined.

The strength of Dominican baseball is found in each of the Major League's 30 teams. And at the same time, baseball is

Nelson Cruz sits on the bench before a game.

like Nelson Cruz keep baseball fever going strong on the island! And that same baseball fever is what helped make Cruz the player he is today.

Early Life

Nelson Cruz was born on July 1, 1980 in Monte Cristi in the Dominican Republic. His father, Nelson Cruz, Sr., played baseball in the Dominican Republic, and he taught his son to love sports too. Nelson, Jr. loved to play basketball and baseball. When he was older,

Nelson even played basketball for the Dominican Junior National team!

Nelson went to high school in Monte Cristi. He played sports all through high school. As he got older, **scouts** from Major League Baseball started to notice Nelson. They saw that he could be a great player one day. They believed that with the right training he could get better and better.

In 1998, when Nelson was only 17, he got his chance to play baseball for a living. On February 23, 1998, the New York Mets

On February 23, 1998, the New York Mets signed a **contract** with Nelson. Nelson wouldn't go right to the minors. The team started Nelson playing in the Dominican Summer Leagues, so that he could get more practice and learn to be an even better player. But he was on his way. Now he just had to work hard and show how good a player he could be.

Nelson spent the next three years playing in the Dominican Summer League, and he got better and better. But he didn't break into the **minor leagues** the way he had been hoping. Then in 2000, the Mets **traded** Nelson to the Oakland Athletics. Nelson wouldn't go to the Mets' minor league teams after all. But the team that brought him into baseball still means a lot to Nelson. Years later, Nelson told a reporter that the Mets would "always be special" to him.

"They signed me," Nelson said. "They taught me everything I know."

The Oakland A's sent Nelson to play in the United States where he would play for one of Oakland's minor league teams. Now he would have to work his way up to playing in the big leagues. But he finally had his chance to play in the MLB.

Nelson had always loved sports, and he finally had a chance to make sports his life. And he wouldn't waste it!

Chapter 2

STARTING IN BASEBALL

In 2001, Cruz played his first season in the minor leagues. He started the 2001 season playing for the Arizona League Athletics (AZL). The team plays in the Rookie League.

Cruz in the Minor Leagues

Cruz played in 23 games for the AZL Athletics in 2001. During that time, Cruz's batting average was .250. He hit 3 home runs and had 16 RBIs.

In 2002, Cruz played for the Vancouver Canadians. Cruz played in 63 games for Vancouver in the 2002 season, and he had 25 RBIs and stole 12 bases. His batting average was .276.

In the outfield, Cruz's fielding percentage was .961.

In the 2003 season, Cruz moved teams again. This time, he played with the Kane County Cougars. In 2003, Cruz also played in 119 games for Kane County. He hit 20 home runs and 85 RBIs. In the outfield, Cruz had 271 putouts, and his fielding percentage was .979.

In 2004, Cruz played for three different minor league teams. He began the season with the Modesto Athletics and played in 66 games for Modesto. He hit 11 home runs and had 52 RBIs, and his batting average with Modesto was .345. Then, after playing for Modesto, Cruz moved to the Midland Rockhounds, a Double-A team. It was a lot of jumping around for Cruz, but he was moving his way up through the minor leagues. Cruz played in 67 games for the Rockhounds, and he hit 14 home runs and had 46 RBIs. Cruz also played a few games for the Sacramento River Cats in 2004, a class-AAA team. Now Cruz had reached the top of the minor leagues.

After the 2004 season, Cruz left Oakland and signed with the Milwaukee

Nelson Cruz
DOMINICAN REPUBLIC

Once Cruz moved from the Rangers to the Brewers, his future started to look very bright.

Brewers. The Brewers sent Cruz to play for their minor league teams. In the 2005 season, Cruz began playing with the Huntsville Stars, a class-AA team that plays in the Southern League. Cruz played in 68 games for Huntsville in 2005 and hit 16 home runs and had 54 RBIs. His batting average was .306.

Next, the Brewers sent Cruz to play with the Nashville Sounds. Nashville is a Triple-A team playing in the Pacific Coast League. Cruz played 60 games for the Sounds in 2005. Cruz's batting average was .269 while playing with Nashville.

Nelson was getting tired of moving from team to team, but he was working hard to improve his performance. Soon, he would finally get his chance to break into the MLB!

Playing in the Majors

In September 2005, Cruz at last got his chance to play in the Majors. The Brewers called Cruz up to play with the team at the end of the 2005 season. Cruz played in just eight games with the Brewers in 2005, but he didn't mind that he didn't get to play much. After all, he had finally reached his dream. He could be patient a little while longer, because he knew the future looked bright.

Chapter 3

MOVING TO
THE RANGERS

I n 2006, Nelson Cruz would get to play in the MLB even more. Cruz was finally reaching his dream of playing in the big leagues.

Playing for Texas

Cruz began the 2006 season playing for the Nashville Sounds. He played 104 games for Nashville in the 2006 season. Cruz hit 20 home runs and had 73 RBIs, and his batting average was .302.

Then, in July 2006, Cruz moved from the Brewers to the Texas Rangers. Cruz played 41 games with the Rangers in the 2006 season, hitting 6 home runs with 22 RBIs and a batting average of .223. Cruz played left, right, and center field for the Rangers. He played right field more than any other position, though, and in right field, Cruz's fielding percentage was 1.000 in 38 games.

The Rangers didn't have the best season in 2006. The team finished third in the American League West *division*, winning 80 games and losing 82. The team finished the season 13 games behind the division leader.

Vladimir Guerrero and Nelson Cruz prepare for a game.

2008 was a hard year for Cruz.

In 2007, Cruz didn't have his best season either. He played in 96 games for Texas, but he hit only 9 home runs and had only 34 RBIs in that time with a batting average of .235. Cruz played both left and right field in 2007, with 82 games in right field. His fielding percentage in right field was .968, and he had 148 putouts.

The Rangers didn't have a great season, either. The team finished last in the AL West, winning only 75 games and losing 87. Texas finished the season 19 games behind the first-place Los Angeles Angels.

Cruz hadn't done as well as he would have liked in 2007. The Rangers wanted Cruz to do better too. In the next season, Cruz would have to show Texas that he really could play in the MLB.

Back to the Minors

In 2008, Cruz had a tough year. Before the season started, he was waived from the Rangers and sent back to the minor leagues. The Rangers just weren't happy with how he had played in 2007, so he would play for the Triple-A Oklahoma Redhawks now, while he worked on his performance.

Cruz played in 103 games for the Redhawks, and he hit 37 home runs and had 99 RBIs during that time, with a batting average of .342. Cruz was doing his best to prove to the Rangers that he had what it took to be a great player. He even won the Pacific Coast League Most Valuable Player Award in 2008.

The Rangers' managers were paying attention. In August, they brought Cruz back up to the Major Leagues, and Cruz played the rest of the season with Texas. In the 31 games he played for the Rangers in 2008, he hit 7 home runs and had 26 RBIs; his batting average was .330.

Now Cruz was ready to stay in the MLB during 2009, too!

Chapter 4

CRUZ COMES BACK

In 2009, Cruz had one of the best years of his career in baseball. He'd had a rough year in 2008, and now he wanted to prove that he belonged in the Majors. In the 2009 season, Cruz got his chance to show how good a player he really could be!

2009 was one of Cruz's best years.

Success with the Rangers

Cruz played in 128 games for the Rangers in 2009. He hit 33 home runs during the season, the most of his career, and he had 76 RBIs and stole 20 bases. His batting average was .260. He started 117 games in right field, and he had 294 putouts. Cruz's fielding percentage was .990 in right field. Cruz also played two games in left field.

Cruz was chosen to replace Torii Hunter in the 2009 All-Star game. He also joined in the Home Run Derby in 2009,

and he did well in the game, too: he finished second to Prince Fielder (from the Milwaukee Brewers). No other player from the American League finished ahead of Cruz.

The Rangers did well in 2009 too. The team finished with 87 wins and 75 losses, second place in the American League West division. Texas was 10 games behind the first-place Los Angeles Angels. The team had done very well during the season—but the Rangers didn't make it to the postseason in 2009.

In 2010, though, things just got better for Cruz and the Rangers. Cruz played in 108 games for the Rangers in the 2010 season, hitting 22 home runs with 78 RBIs and a batting average of .318. He played left and right field again—in left field for 14 games and right field for 94 games. In right field, Cruz had 228 putouts, and his fielding percentage was .979.

The Rangers had a great year! The team finished first in the AL West division with 90 wins and 72 losses. The team was 9 games ahead of the second-place Oakland Athletics.

In the American League Division Series, the Rangers played the Tampa Bay Rays in a series that lasted for five games. In the end, the Rangers won Game 5 and beat the Rays. The Rangers went on from

In 2010, things got better for Cruz and the Rangers.

Sadly, Cruz and the Rangers went back to Texas without winning the World Series.

there to play the Yankees in the American League Championship Series. After six games, the Rangers beat the Yankees.

Texas was headed to the World Series!

The Rangers played against the San Francisco Giants in the 2010 World Series. The Giants won the first two games.

Things looked bad for the Rangers. Texas won Game 3, but the Giants won the next two games. The Rangers had lost the World Series. Cruz and the Rangers were headed back to Texas without a World Series Championship.

Chapter 5

NELSON CRUZ TODAY

Cruz was ready to help his team get another shot at the World Series. Only this time, he hoped they'd finish the Series as champions.

Cruz's Biggest Year Yet

Cruz got a big start to the 2011 season. He hit a home run in the first four games of the season. Only Willie Mays and Mark McGwire had done the same thing! And he played well for the rest of the regular season. In the 124 games he played for the Rangers, Cruz hit 29 home runs and had 87 RBIs. His batting average was .263 for the 2011 regular season.

The Rangers did very well in 2011 too, finishing first in the American League West division. Texas had won 96 games and lost just 66 in the regular season. The second-place Angels were 10 games behind the Rangers at the end of the season.

In the American League Division Series, the Rangers played the Tampa Bay Rays. The Rays won the first game of the series—but the Rangers won the next three. They had won the series again!

Then Rangers played the Detroit Tigers in the 2011 American League Championship Series. Texas beat Detroit in the first game of the series, 3–2. Game 2 of the series was tied going into the 11th inning, and the game had gone on for more than four hours. Then Cruz took the plate and hit a walk-off grand slam. The game was over—and the Rangers had

won! Fireworks lit up the sky above the stadium in Arlington, Texas, and the fans in the crowd cheered as loudly as they could. No other player in history has ever hit a walk-off grand slam in a postseason game. Cruz had made history. And he'd won the game for Texas!

In Game 4, Cruz hit a three-run home run and helped win the game for the Rangers. The Rangers beat the Tigers in Game 5, too. Texas won the series. After the series was over, Cruz was named 2011 ALCS MVP. Cruz couldn't have been happier.

"When the team needed me, I delivered," he told fans and reporters. "It was amazing."

The Rangers went on to the World Series for the second year in a row. This time Texas played the St. Louis Cardinals. The series went all the way to Game 7. The last game of the series was close. But in the end, the Cardinals beat the Rangers. Texas had lost another World Series.

Cruz had still had an amazing season, though. He had helped bring the Rangers to the World Series again. He'd been named ALCS MVP. His postseason play broke more than one record. No player has ever hit more home runs or had more RBIs in a postseason series than Cruz. His fans will never forget Cruz's 2011 season!

After his long career in baseball, Cruz had reached the top of the sport. Cruz had worked for years in the minors. He'd gotten better and better over time. And now, he was showing the world how great a player he was. No other player in history had done the things Cruz had. Nelson Cruz proves that when you try your best, amazing things can happen!

Life Outside Baseball

Nelson Cruz has had a wonderful career in baseball. He's played in the World Series. He's played in the All-Star game. He has hit more than 100 home runs. No player in the MLB has hit more home runs or had more RBIs in one postseason series. In the 2011 ALCS, Cruz proved how great a player he really is.

But the sport he loves isn't the only thing that's important to Cruz. In 2009, Cruz and Solani Genao were married on December 25. Starting a family of his own was a big step for Nelson Cruz. But he was ready to build a family.

Nelson has worked hard, but he's also had good luck. He's been very blessed,

Nelson Cruz has had an amazing baseball career.

and now he wants to giving back to others. That is a big part of Cruz's life, too. He has worked hard to share his success with others. He helps kids see dentists when their families wouldn't be able to afford it otherwise. He's talked with young people playing baseball in the Dominican Republic, too, sharing his story with them and encouraging them to do their best to work hard and improve themselves. In 2010, Cruz even won an award for his work to help kids!

Cruz has done great things in baseball. But his work for others is even greater.

And fans will keep watching Cruz to see what he will do next!

Find Out More

Online

Baseball Almanac
www.baseball-almanac.com

Baseball Hall of Fame
baseballhall.org

Baseball Reference
www.baseball-reference.com

Dominican Baseball
mlb.mlb.com/mlb/features/dr/index.jsp

History of Baseball
www.19cbaseball.com/

Major League Baseball
www.mlb.com

Science of Baseball
www.exploratorium.edu/baseball/

In Books

Augustin, Bryan. *The Dominican Republic From A to Z.* New York: Scholastic, 2005.

Jacobs, Greg. *The Everything Kids' Baseball Book.* Avon, Mass.: F+W Media, Inc. 2012.

Kurlansky, Mark. *The Eastern Stars: How Baseball Changed the Dominican Town of San Pedro de Macorís.* New York: Riverhead Books, 2010.

Glossary

All-Star Game: The game played in July between the best players from each of the two leagues within the MLB.

batting average: A statistic that measures how good a batter is, which is calculated by dividing the number of hits a player gets by how many times he is at bat.

contract: A written promise between a player and the team. It tells how much he will be paid for how long.

culture: The way of life of a group of people, which includes things like values and beliefs, language, food, and art.

defense: Playing to keep the other team from scoring; includes the outfield and infield positions, pitcher, and catcher.

disabled list: A list of players who are injured and can't play for a certain period of time.

division: A group of teams that plays one another to compete for the championship; in the MLB, divisions are based on geographic regions.

free agent: A player who does not currently have a contract with any team.

general manager: The person in charge of a baseball team, who is responsible for guiding the team to do well.

heritage: Something passed down by previous generations.

Major League Baseball (MLB): The highest level of professional baseball in the United States and Canada.

minor leagues: The level of professional baseball right below the Major Leagues.

Most Valuable Player (MVP): The athlete who is named the best player for a certain period of time.

offense: Playing to score runs at bat.

playoffs: A series of games played after the regular season ends, to determine who will win the championship.

professional: The level of baseball in which players get paid.

rookie: A player in his first-year in the MLB.

runs batted in (RBI): The number of points that a player gets for his team by hitting the ball.

scouts: People who find the best young baseball players to sign to teams.

sign: To agree to a contract between a baseball player and a team.

trade: An agreement with another team that gives a player in return for a player from the other team.

Index